I0504858

CREATING FINANCIAL FREEDOM

Your Blueprint to Multiple Income Streams (MSIs)

Patil A

Copyright © 2023 Patil A

All rights reserved

The characters and events portrayed in this book are fictitious. Any similarity to real persons, living or dead, is coincidental and not intended by the author.

No part of this book may be reproduced, or stored in a retrieval system, or transmitted in any form or by any means, electronic, mechanical, photocopying, recording, or otherwise, without express written permission of the publisher.

ISBN: 9798394142628

Table of Contents

INTRODUCTION

For many people, the idea of financial freedom can seem like an unattainable dream. It's easy to get caught up in the daily grind of work and bills, without taking the time to consider the long-term impact on our finances. However, achieving financial freedom is not only possible, but it can also be the key to unlocking a life of abundance, opportunity, and fulfillment.

Creating Financial Freedom: Your Blueprint to Multiple Income Streams is designed to help you do just that. In this book, you'll learn how to build a sustainable income portfolio that includes multiple income streams. Whether you're just starting out or you're a seasoned entrepreneur, this book will provide you with the tools, strategies, and mindset needed to take your finances to the next level.

First, we'll explore why financial freedom is so important. Financial freedom gives you the power to make choices that align with your values and goals, rather than being tied down by financial constraints. It allows you to pursue your passions, travel the world, and spend more time with loved ones. It also provides a sense of security and peace of mind, knowing that you have a cushion to fall back on in case of unexpected expenses or job loss.

Next, we'll dive into the concept of income streams. We'll explore the various types of income streams, including active income, passive income, and portfolio income. We'll also discuss the importance of diversifying your income streams to minimize risk and maximize earning potential.

From there, we'll cover a range of strategies for building multiple income streams. These include leveraging your skills and talents, creating passive income streams through investments and real estate, building an online business through affiliate marketing, digital products, and e-commerce, and pursuing freelance or consulting work. We'll also explore the benefits and pitfalls of network marketing and multi-level marketing, as well as the power of building a successful YouTube channel or podcast.

Finally, we'll discuss the importance of building a personal brand to achieve long-term financial success. Your personal brand is what sets you apart from others and positions you as an expert in your field. It allows you to build a loyal following and create multiple income streams through collaborations, sponsorships, and product sales.

By the end of this book, you'll have a solid understanding of how to create financial freedom through multiple income streams. You'll have the knowledge and tools needed to build a sustainable income portfolio that provides you with the freedom and flexibility to live life on your own terms. So, let's get started on the journey to financial freedom!

CHAPTER 1: THE IMPORTANCE OF FINANCIAL FREEDOM

Financial freedom is a term that is often used, but what exactly does it mean? Financial freedom is the ability to live life on your own terms, without being held back by financial constraints. It means having the freedom to pursue your passions, travel, spend time with loved ones, and make choices that align with your values and goals. Financial freedom provides a sense of security and peace of mind, knowing that you have a cushion to fall back on in case of unexpected expenses or job loss.

The importance of financial freedom cannot be overstated. Here are a few reasons why achieving financial freedom should be a top priority:

1. You can pursue your passions

One of the biggest benefits of financial freedom is that it allows you to pursue your passions. When you're not tied down by financial constraints, you can take risks and pursue projects that you're truly passionate about. This can lead to a sense of fulfillment and purpose that is hard to achieve when you're simply working to pay the bills.

2. You can travel the world

Travel is one of the most enriching experiences you can have in life. However, it can be difficult to travel when you're tied to a 9-5 job and limited vacation time. Financial freedom allows you to travel more frequently and for longer periods of time, giving you the opportunity to explore new cultures, meet new people, and expand your horizons.

3. You can spend more time with loved ones

Spending time with loved ones is one of life's greatest joys. Unfortunately, work and financial constraints can often get in the way of spending quality time with family and friends. Financial freedom provides the flexibility to prioritize your relationships and spend more time with the people who matter most to you.

4. You have a safety net

Unexpected expenses can be a major source of stress and anxiety. Whether it's a medical emergency, a car repair, or a job loss, having a safety net in the form of savings or passive income can provide peace of mind and reduce stress. Financial freedom means having the security of a safety net, which can help you weather unexpected challenges with greater ease.

5. You can retire comfortably

Retirement is something that we all look forward to, but many people worry about whether they will have enough money to retire comfortably. Achieving financial freedom means having the ability to retire on your own terms, without worrying about whether you will have enough money to support yourself in your golden years.

In conclusion, achieving financial freedom is not just about having more money. It's about having the freedom to live life on your own terms, pursue your passions, and spend time with loved ones. It's about having the security and peace of mind that comes from knowing that you have a safety net in case of unexpected expenses or job loss. In the following chapters, we'll explore strategies for building multiple income streams that can help you achieve the financial freedom you deserve.

CHAPTER 2: UNDERSTANDING INCOME STREAMS

Creating multiple income streams is an essential step towards achieving financial freedom. But before we dive into the strategies for building these income streams, it's important to understand what income streams are and why they are important.

What are income streams?

Income streams refer to the different sources of money that you have coming in. Most people have a primary source of income, such as a full-time job, but creating additional income streams can provide greater financial security and flexibility. There are two types of income streams:

Active income streams

Active income streams refer to money that you earn through active work, such as a salary from a job, freelance work, or consulting services. Active income streams require you to exchange your time and energy for money, and they are typically limited by the number of hours you can work in a day.

Passive income streams

Passive income streams refer to money that you earn without

actively working for it. These can include rental income, dividends from investments, royalties from creative work, or income from a business that runs without your day-to-day involvement. Passive income streams require an initial investment of time and resources to set up, but they can provide a steady stream of income over time.

Why are income streams important?

Creating multiple income streams is important for several reasons:

Diversification

Having multiple income streams provides diversification, which can help reduce risk and increase financial stability. If one income stream dries up, you have others to fall back on.

Flexibility

Having multiple income streams provides greater flexibility in terms of how you spend your time and where you work. You're not tied to one job or one income source, which gives you greater control over your schedule and your financial future.

Increased income

Creating multiple income streams can provide a significant increase in income, which can help you achieve your financial goals more quickly.

Security

Having multiple income streams provides greater financial security, which can help reduce stress and anxiety. If one income stream is affected by economic or other external factors, you have others to rely on.

In conclusion, understanding income streams is an important step towards achieving financial freedom. By diversifying your income sources, you can increase financial stability, flexibility, and security, while also providing opportunities for increased income. In the following chapters, we'll explore specific strategies for building both active and passive income streams that can help you achieve the financial freedom you desire.

CHAPTER 3: LEVERAGING YOUR SKILLS AND TALENTS

One of the most effective ways to create multiple income streams is to leverage your existing skills and talents. Whether you have expertise in a particular industry, a creative talent, or a specific set of skills, there are a variety of ways to turn your abilities into additional income streams. In this chapter, we'll explore some strategies for leveraging your skills and talents to create new income streams.

Identify your skills and talents

The first step in leveraging your skills and talents is to identify what you're good at. This can include anything from writing and graphic design to programming, photography, or public speaking. You may already have a full-time job that utilizes some of these skills, but there are likely opportunities to use them in different ways to create additional income streams.

Once you've identified your skills and talents, it's important to determine which ones are in demand and how you can monetize them. This may require some research into your industry or niche to see what types of services or products are needed.

Create a portfolio

To market your skills and talents effectively, you'll need to create a portfolio that showcases your work. This can include examples of your writing, design work, programming projects, or any other relevant work you've done. A portfolio can be as simple as a website or blog that showcases your work, or it can be a more comprehensive document that includes detailed descriptions of your skills and experience.

Market your skills and talents

Once you have a portfolio in place, it's time to start marketing your skills and talents. There are a variety of ways to do this, depending on your niche and target audience. Some options include:

- **Freelancing websites:** Platforms like Upwork, Fiverr, and Freelancer allow you to create a profile and bid on projects that match your skills.
- **Social media:** Use social media to share your portfolio and showcase your work. You can also join groups and communities related to your niche to connect with potential clients.
- **Referrals:** Ask satisfied clients to refer you to others who may need your services.
- **Networking:** Attend industry events and meetups to connect with potential clients and collaborators.

Create digital products

Another way to monetize your skills and talents is by creating digital products like ebooks, courses, or templates. For example, if you're a graphic designer, you could create a set of templates for social media posts or marketing materials. If you're a writer, you could create an ebook or online course on a topic related to your niche.

Digital products can provide a passive income stream once they're created, as people can purchase them without any additional effort on your part. This can be a great way to supplement your active income streams.

In conclusion, leveraging your skills and talents is an effective way to create multiple income streams. By identifying what you're good at, creating a portfolio, and marketing your skills effectively, you can tap into a variety of opportunities to monetize your expertise. Whether you choose to freelance, create digital products, or pursue other opportunities, leveraging your skills and talents can provide a solid foundation for financial freedom.

CHAPTER 4: CREATING PASSIVE INCOME STREAMS

Passive income streams are a great way to generate income without requiring constant effort or time investment. In this chapter, we'll explore some strategies for creating passive income streams.

What is Passive Income?

Passive income is income that is earned without any active involvement from you. This means that you're earning money while you sleep, travel, or spend time with your family. Examples of passive income streams include rental income, dividends from stocks, and royalties from books or music.

Invest in Rental Properties

One way to create passive income streams is to invest in rental properties. This can be a great way to generate income from a property that you own without having to actively manage it on a day-to-day basis. Of course, there are some risks associated with owning rental properties, so it's important to do your research and understand the market before investing.

Dividend Stocks

Another way to generate passive income is to invest in dividend-paying stocks. Dividends are payments made to shareholders by a company, and they can provide a steady stream of income over time. While there is some risk associated with investing in the stock market, dividend stocks can provide a relatively stable source of passive income.

Create and Sell Digital Products

Creating and selling digital products can also be a great way to generate passive income. This could include anything from ebooks and online courses to stock photos or printables. Once you've created a digital product, you can sell it on platforms like Etsy or Gumroad without any additional effort on your part.

Affiliate Marketing

Affiliate marketing is a popular way to generate passive income online. This involves promoting other people's products or services through your website or social media channels. When someone clicks on your affiliate link and makes a purchase, you earn a commission. While it can take time and effort to build a strong affiliate marketing strategy, it can provide a consistent source of passive income over time.

Create a Productized Service

A productized service is a service that's packaged like a product. This means that it's standardized and has a fixed price, making it easier to sell and scale. Productized services can include anything from social media management to website design. By creating a productized service, you can generate passive income by selling your services without having to actively manage each project.

In conclusion, creating passive income streams can be an effective way to generate income without requiring constant effort or time investment. By investing in rental properties, dividend-paying stocks, or creating and selling digital products, you can build a foundation for passive income. Affiliate marketing and creating a productized service can also be great options for generating passive income. While it may take time and effort to establish passive income streams, the long-term benefits can be well worth it.

CHAPTER 5:
INVESTING FOR
MULTIPLE INCOME
STREAMS

Investing is a powerful tool for creating multiple income streams. By investing in a variety of assets, you can diversify your income and reduce your overall risk. In this chapter, we'll explore some strategies for investing in a way that creates multiple income streams.

What is Investing for Multiple Income Streams?

Investing for multiple income streams involves investing in assets that generate income. This income can come in the form of dividends, interest payments, rental income, or capital gains. By investing in a variety of assets that generate income, you can create multiple income streams that provide a steady flow of money.

Diversify Your Portfolio

The first step in investing for multiple income streams is to diversify your portfolio. This means investing in a variety of assets, such as stocks, bonds, real estate, and alternative investments. By diversifying your portfolio, you can reduce your overall risk and ensure that you have multiple sources of income.

Dividend Stocks

One way to invest for multiple income streams is to focus on dividend-paying stocks. Dividend stocks are stocks that pay a portion of their profits back to shareholders in the form of dividends. By investing in a variety of dividend-paying stocks, you can create a steady stream of income from your portfolio.

Real Estate

Real estate is another asset class that can provide multiple income streams. By investing in rental properties, you can generate rental income on a monthly basis. Additionally, real estate can appreciate in value over time, providing capital gains if you choose to sell your properties in the future.

Bonds

Bonds are debt securities that are issued by companies or governments. By investing in bonds, you can earn interest payments on a regular basis. While bonds typically provide lower returns than stocks or real estate, they can be a good option for investors who want to reduce their overall risk.

Alternative Investments

Finally, alternative investments can also provide multiple income streams. Alternative investments can include anything from private equity and hedge funds to commodities and cryptocurrencies. While alternative investments can be riskier than traditional investments, they can also provide higher returns.

In conclusion, investing for multiple income streams involves diversifying your portfolio and investing in a variety of assets that generate income. By focusing on dividend-paying stocks, real estate, bonds, and alternative investments, you can create multiple sources of income that provide a steady flow of money. While investing always involves risk, the potential rewards of investing for multiple income streams can be significant.

CHAPTER 6: REAL ESTATE INVESTMENT STRATEGIES

Real estate investment can be a powerful way to generate multiple income streams. Whether you are interested in rental properties, fix-and-flips, or long-term investment strategies, real estate can provide a variety of opportunities to create wealth. In this chapter, we'll explore some real estate investment strategies that you can use to generate multiple income streams.

Rental Properties

One of the most popular real estate investment strategies is rental properties. Rental properties involve purchasing a property and renting it out to tenants. The rental income can provide a steady stream of cash flow, while the property can appreciate in value over time.

When investing in rental properties, it's important to consider factors such as location, rental rates, and potential repair costs. Additionally, you'll need to manage the property, either on your own or by hiring a property manager.

Fix-and-Flips

Fix-and-flips involve purchasing a property, renovating it, and then selling it for a profit. This strategy can provide quick returns, but it also involves a higher level of risk. To be successful with fix-and-flips, you'll need to accurately estimate renovation costs and market the property effectively to potential buyers.

Long-Term Investment

Long-term real estate investment involves purchasing a property with the intention of holding it for an extended period of time. This strategy can provide a steady stream of rental income, as well as potential appreciation in property value over time. To be successful with long-term investment, it's important to carefully consider factors such as location, market trends, and potential repair costs.

REITs

Real estate investment trusts (REITs) are a type of investment that allows investors to own shares in a portfolio of properties. REITs can provide a diversified investment portfolio that generates income through rental income and property appreciation. Additionally, REITs can be a more liquid investment, as shares can be bought and sold on stock exchanges.

Real Estate Crowdfunding

Real estate crowdfunding involves pooling money from multiple investors to fund a real estate project. This strategy can provide access to larger real estate projects that may be out of reach for individual investors. Additionally, real estate crowdfunding can provide a passive income stream, as the investment is managed by the crowdfunding platform.

In conclusion, real estate investment can provide a variety of strategies to generate multiple income streams. Whether you are interested in rental properties, fix-and-flips, or long-term investment, there are opportunities to create wealth through real estate investment. By carefully considering factors such as location, market trends, and potential repair costs, you can find a real estate investment strategy that works for you.

CHAPTER 7: BUILDING AN ONLINE BUSINESS

In today's digital age, building an online business can provide a powerful way to generate multiple income streams. Whether you're interested in e-commerce, affiliate marketing, or online education, there are a variety of opportunities to create wealth through online entrepreneurship. In this chapter, we'll explore some strategies for building a successful online business.

Choose a Niche

The first step in building an online business is to choose a niche. A niche is a specific area of interest or expertise that you can focus on in your business. Choosing a niche can help you differentiate yourself from competitors and build a loyal audience.

When choosing a niche, consider factors such as your interests, skills, and market demand. Additionally, research your potential competitors to see what they are offering and how you can differentiate yourself.

Create a Website

Once you have chosen a niche, the next step is to create a website. A website can serve as the hub of your online business, providing a place for potential customers to learn about your products or services.

When creating a website, consider factors such as design, functionality, and search engine optimization (SEO). Additionally, ensure that your website is mobile-friendly, as an increasing number of consumers access the internet through mobile devices.

Attract Traffic

After creating a website, the next step is to attract traffic. Traffic refers to the number of people who visit your website. There are a variety of strategies for attracting traffic, including search engine optimization (SEO), social media marketing, and paid advertising.

When attracting traffic, it's important to focus on your target audience. Consider factors such as their interests, demographics, and behaviors. Additionally, track your website analytics to determine which strategies are most effective.

Monetize Your Website

The final step in building an online business is to monetize your website. Monetization refers to the process of earning revenue from your website. There are a variety of strategies for monetizing your website, including e-commerce, affiliate marketing, and online courses.

When monetizing your website, consider factors such as your target audience, pricing, and marketing strategies. Additionally, focus on providing value to your customers and building a loyal audience.

In conclusion, building an online business can provide a powerful way to generate multiple income streams. By choosing a niche, creating a website, attracting traffic, and monetizing your website, you can build a successful online business that provides a steady stream of income. With the increasing number of consumers accessing the internet, there has never been a better time to start an online business.

CHAPTER 8: AFFILIATE MARKETING FOR BEGINNERS

Affiliate marketing is a type of online marketing where businesses reward affiliates for promoting their products or services. It's a popular way for individuals to generate passive income streams and can be an excellent option for beginners looking to start an online business. In this chapter, we'll explore some tips and strategies for getting started with affiliate marketing.

Understand the Basics

Before getting started with affiliate marketing, it's important to understand the basics. Affiliate marketing involves promoting a product or service and earning a commission for each sale made through your unique affiliate link. The commission rate can vary depending on the product or service being promoted.

Additionally, it's important to understand the different types of affiliate marketing, including pay-per-click (PPC), pay-per-lead (PPL), and pay-per-sale (PPS). Each type of affiliate marketing has different commission structures and can require different strategies for success.

Choose a Niche

Like with any online business, choosing a niche is important for success in affiliate marketing. When choosing a niche, consider factors such as your interests, expertise, and market demand. Additionally, research potential affiliate programs to see what products or services align with your niche and have high commission rates.

Find Affiliate Programs

After choosing a niche, the next step is to find affiliate programs. There are a variety of affiliate programs available, including those offered by individual companies and third-party platforms such as Amazon Associates and ShareASale.

When choosing an affiliate program, consider factors such as commission rates, payment options, and program requirements. Additionally, research the reputation of the affiliate program to ensure it's a trustworthy and reliable option.

Create Content

Once you have found an affiliate program, the next step is to create content to promote the products or services. This can include blog posts, social media posts, and email marketing campaigns.

When creating content, focus on providing value to your audience and promoting products or services that align with their interests and needs. Additionally, ensure that you disclose your affiliate relationship to your audience to maintain transparency and trust.

Track Your Performance

The final step in affiliate marketing is to track your performance. This can include monitoring clicks, conversions, and earnings. By tracking your performance, you can identify which strategies are most effective and make adjustments to optimize your success.

In conclusion, affiliate marketing can be an excellent option for beginners looking to start an online business. By understanding the basics, choosing a niche, finding affiliate programs, creating content, and tracking your performance, you can build a successful affiliate marketing business and generate passive income streams.

CHAPTER 9: CREATING DIGITAL PRODUCTS

Digital products have become increasingly popular in recent years, as more individuals are looking for ways to generate passive income streams online. Creating digital products can be an excellent option for those looking to start an online business, as it allows for scalability and low overhead costs. In this chapter, we'll explore some tips and strategies for creating digital products.

Identify Your Niche and Audience

Like with any online business, identifying your niche and audience is crucial for success in creating digital products. When choosing a niche, consider your interests, expertise, and market demand. Additionally, research potential audiences to see what types of digital products they may be interested in.

Choose a Digital Product Type

There are a variety of digital product types to choose from, including e-books, online courses, software, and digital art. When choosing a digital product type, consider your skills, expertise, and audience. Additionally, research potential competitors to see what types of digital products are successful in your niche.

Plan and Outline Your Product

Once you have identified your niche, audience, and digital product type, the next step is to plan and outline your product. This can include creating a content outline, developing a timeline, and creating a budget.

When planning and outlining your product, focus on providing value to your audience and ensuring that your product is unique and stands out from potential competitors. Additionally, consider the format and delivery method for your digital product, such as a downloadable file or an online course platform.

Create Your Product

After planning and outlining your digital product, the next step is to create it. This can involve writing content, designing graphics, developing software, or recording video content.

When creating your product, focus on quality and ensuring that it aligns with your outlined plan. Additionally, consider user experience and make sure that your digital product is easy to navigate and understand.

Market and Sell Your Product

Once your digital product is created, the final step is to market and sell it. This can involve creating a sales page, promoting your product on social media, and utilizing email marketing campaigns.

When marketing and selling your product, focus on providing value to potential customers and highlighting the unique aspects of your product. Additionally, consider offering promotions or discounts to incentivize sales.

In conclusion, creating digital products can be an excellent option for those looking to generate passive income streams online. By identifying your niche and audience, choosing a digital product type, planning and outlining your product, creating it, and marketing and selling it, you can build a successful digital product business and generate passive income streams.

CHAPTER 10: DROPSHIPPING AND E-COMMERCE

Dropshipping and e-commerce are two popular business models that have gained popularity in recent years. They both offer opportunities for individuals to start an online business without the need for physical inventory or a brick-and-mortar storefront. In this chapter, we'll explore the basics of dropshipping and e-commerce and some tips for success in each model.

Dropshipping

Dropshipping is a business model where a seller does not hold any inventory, but instead, partners with a supplier who handles the product fulfillment and shipping. The seller simply takes orders from customers and passes them on to the supplier, who then ships the product directly to the customer.

One of the primary advantages of dropshipping is the low upfront cost. With no need for physical inventory or a storefront, starting a dropshipping business can be done with minimal capital. Additionally, the lack of inventory management and shipping logistics can save time and resources for the seller.

To be successful in dropshipping, it's important to choose a profitable niche and partner with reliable suppliers. Additionally, optimizing your online store for conversions and investing in marketing efforts can help drive traffic and sales.

E-commerce

E-commerce, on the other hand, involves selling physical products through an online store. Unlike dropshipping, the seller holds inventory and is responsible for order fulfillment and shipping.

One of the primary advantages of e-commerce is the ability to control the product inventory and customer experience. Additionally, owning the inventory can allow for more flexibility in product pricing and bundling.

To be successful in e-commerce, it's important to choose a profitable niche and source products from reliable suppliers. Additionally, optimizing your online store for conversions, investing in marketing efforts, and providing excellent customer service can help drive traffic and sales.

Combining Dropshipping and E-commerce

While dropshipping and e-commerce are distinct business models, they can also be combined to create a hybrid model. This can involve holding some inventory while also dropshipping certain products.

By combining the two models, a seller can take advantage of the benefits of each, such as the low upfront cost of dropshipping and the control over inventory and pricing in e-commerce. However, it's important to carefully manage the inventory and fulfillment process to ensure timely and accurate delivery to customers.

In conclusion, dropshipping and e-commerce are two popular business models that offer opportunities for individuals to start an online business. While each has its unique advantages and challenges, combining the two models can provide a hybrid approach to building a successful online store. By choosing a profitable niche, sourcing reliable products, optimizing for conversions, and investing in marketing efforts, individuals can build a successful dropshipping or e-commerce business.

CHAPTER 11:
FREELANCING AND
CONSULTING

Freelancing and consulting are two popular ways to earn money while utilizing your skills and expertise. Both offer a great opportunity to create a flexible work schedule and have control over your income streams.

Freelancing involves offering your services as a self-employed professional to clients who need them. This can range from writing and editing to web design, graphic design, social media management, and more. As a freelancer, you can choose which projects to take on and set your own rates.

Consulting, on the other hand, involves offering your expertise in a particular field to businesses or individuals who need guidance. This could include areas such as marketing, finance, human resources, or management. As a consultant, you can help clients develop strategies and solutions to improve their business.

Here are some steps to get started with freelancing and consulting:

Identify your skills and expertise: Freelancing and consulting require a specific skill set, so it's important to identify what you're good at and what you can offer to clients.

Build your portfolio: Your portfolio is your chance to showcase your skills and expertise to potential clients. This could be a website, social media profiles, or samples of your work.

Establish your rates: Determine how much you want to charge for your services. This can vary depending on the type of work you're doing and your experience level.

Find clients: There are a variety of ways to find clients, including through networking, social media, job boards, and freelance marketplaces.

Deliver quality work: Once you have clients, it's important to deliver quality work and meet deadlines. This will help you build a positive reputation and establish long-term relationships with clients.

Grow your business: As you gain experience and establish yourself as a freelancer or consultant, you can start to grow your business by increasing your rates, expanding your services, and finding new clients.

Freelancing and consulting can be a great way to earn money while utilizing your skills and expertise. However, it's important to remember that it can take time to build a client base and establish yourself in these fields. With patience, persistence, and hard work, you can create a successful freelancing or consulting business and enjoy the benefits of multiple income streams.

CHAPTER 12:
NETWORK MARKETING AND MULTI-LEVEL MARKETING

Network marketing and multi-level marketing (MLM) are often used interchangeably, but they are slightly different business models. Both involve selling products or services and building a team of distributors, but the main difference is in how distributors are compensated.

In network marketing, distributors earn commissions on the products they sell, as well as bonuses for building a team of other distributors. In MLM, distributors earn commissions not only on their own sales, but also on the sales of their downline (the team they have built).

Both network marketing and MLM can be a great way to earn income while working from home and building a flexible schedule. However, it's important to do your research and choose a company that aligns with your values and offers quality products or services.

Here are some steps to get started with network marketing or MLM:

Research companies: Look for companies that offer quality products or services that you believe in. It's important to choose a company with a good reputation and a proven track record.

Evaluate compensation plans: Each company will have a different compensation plan, so it's important to understand how you will be paid and what you need to do to earn commissions and bonuses.

Join a team: Network marketing and MLM are often done in teams, so it's important to find a team that you can work well with and that offers support and training.

Build your business: To be successful in network marketing or MLM, you will need to build your business by promoting products or services, recruiting new distributors, and training your team.

Stay committed: Building a successful network marketing or MLM business takes time and effort. It's important to stay committed and consistent in your efforts to see results.

Follow ethical practices: Network marketing and MLM have been criticized in the past for unethical practices such as pyramid schemes. It's important to follow ethical practices and ensure that you are not taking advantage of others in your efforts to build your business.

Network marketing and MLM can be a great way to create a secondary income stream while working from home and building a flexible schedule. However, it's important to do your due diligence and choose a reputable company with quality products or services. With hard work and dedication, you can build a successful network marketing or MLM business and enjoy the benefits of multiple income streams.

CHAPTER 13: CREATING A SUCCESSFUL YOUTUBE CHANNEL

YouTube has become one of the most popular platforms for creating and sharing video content. It's not just a place to watch funny cat videos or music videos, but it can also be a powerful tool to build a following, establish yourself as an expert in your field, and generate income through multiple income streams. In this chapter, we'll discuss how to create a successful YouTube channel that attracts viewers and earns you money.

Define your niche: The first step to creating a successful YouTube channel is to define your niche. You want to create content that is unique, relevant, and engaging to your target audience. Whether it's cooking, fitness, beauty, or technology, pick a niche that you are passionate about and that you have expertise in.

Create high-quality content: Once you have identified your niche, it's time to start creating content. The key to creating a successful YouTube channel is to create high-quality content that is valuable and engaging to your viewers. Make sure your videos are well-produced, with good lighting and sound, and that they provide value to your audience.

Optimize your videos for search: YouTube is the second largest search engine in the world, so it's important to optimize your videos for search. Use relevant keywords in your video titles, descriptions, and tags to increase the visibility of your videos in search results.

Engage with your audience: Engagement is key to building a successful YouTube channel. Respond to comments on your videos and engage with your audience on social media platforms. This will help you build a loyal fan base and keep your viewers coming back for more.

Monetize your channel: Once you have built a loyal following and have a good amount of views and subscribers, you can start monetizing your channel. You can make money through multiple income streams such as advertising revenue, sponsorships, affiliate marketing, and selling your own products or merchandise.

Collaborate with other YouTubers: Collaborating with other YouTubers can help you grow your channel and reach a wider audience. Find other creators in your niche and reach out to them for potential collaborations. This can be in the form of guest appearances, joint videos, or promotions.

Consistency is key: Finally, consistency is key to building a successful YouTube channel. You need to be consistent in your content creation and upload schedule. This will help you build a loyal following and keep your viewers engaged and coming back for more.

In conclusion, creating a successful YouTube channel requires hard work, dedication, and persistence. By following these tips, you can create a channel that attracts viewers and generates income through multiple income streams. Remember to define your niche, create high-quality content, optimize your videos for search, engage with your audience, monetize your channel, collaborate with other YouTubers, and be consistent in your content creation.

CHAPTER 14:
THE POWER OF PODCASTING

Podcasting has become a popular medium for individuals to share their thoughts and ideas with others. It allows people to listen to content at their convenience and provides a platform for hosts to reach a global audience. In this chapter, we will discuss the power of podcasting and how it can be used to create multiple income streams.

What is Podcasting?

Podcasting is a form of digital media that consists of an episodic series of audio or video files that a user can download and listen to. It is similar to a radio show, but with the added benefit of being able to listen to content at any time. Podcasts can cover a wide range of topics, from news and politics to entertainment and education.

The Power of Podcasting

Podcasting has become a powerful tool for individuals to reach a large audience and create a loyal following. It provides an opportunity for hosts to share their knowledge and expertise with others and establish themselves as experts in their field.

Here are some of the benefits of podcasting:

Reach a Global Audience: Podcasting allows hosts to reach a global audience, providing an opportunity to share their message with people from all over the world.

Build a Loyal Following: Podcasting allows hosts to connect with their audience on a deeper level, building a loyal following that can lead to greater opportunities in the future.

Establish Yourself as an Expert: Hosting a podcast provides an opportunity for hosts to establish themselves as experts in their field, creating greater credibility and visibility for their brand.

Monetization Opportunities: Podcasting provides several monetization opportunities, including sponsorships, affiliate marketing, and selling products and services.

Creating a Successful Podcast

Creating a successful podcast requires more than just recording and uploading content. It takes time and effort to build an audience and establish yourself as an expert in your field.

Here are some tips for creating a successful podcast:

Choose a Niche: Select a niche that aligns with your interests and expertise. This will help you create content that resonates with your audience and establishes you as an expert in your field.

Invest in Quality Equipment: Invest in quality equipment, including a good microphone and editing software, to ensure that your content is of high quality.

Consistency is Key: Consistency is key when it comes to podcasting. Stick to a regular publishing schedule to keep your audience engaged and interested in your content.

Promote Your Podcast: Promote your podcast on social media, your website, and other platforms to reach a wider audience and attract new listeners.

Monetizing Your Podcast

Podcasting provides several monetization opportunities, including sponsorships, affiliate marketing, and selling products and services. Here are some ways to monetize your podcast:

Sponsorships: Sponsorships involve partnering with companies or brands that align with your niche to promote their products or services.

Affiliate Marketing: Affiliate marketing involves promoting products or services and receiving a commission for each sale made through your unique affiliate link.

Selling Products and Services: Selling products and services, such as courses or coaching, can provide a steady stream of income for podcast hosts.

Podcasting provides a powerful platform for individuals to share their knowledge and expertise with a global audience. It requires time and effort to create a successful podcast, but the benefits are worth the investment. By choosing a niche, investing in quality equipment, promoting your podcast, and monetizing your content, you can create a successful podcast and generate multiple income streams.

CHAPTER 15: BUILDING A BRAND FOR LONG-TERM FINANCIAL SUCCESS

In today's highly competitive market, building a brand is more important than ever. A strong brand can help you stand out from the crowd, build customer loyalty, and ultimately drive long-term financial success. In this chapter, we'll discuss the importance of building a brand and provide practical tips for creating a strong brand that can withstand the test of time.

Why Building a Brand is Important

Building a brand is not just about creating a logo or a catchy tagline. It's about creating a perception of your business in the minds of your customers.

A strong brand can help you:

Establish Credibility: A strong brand helps you establish credibility and trust with your customers. It shows that you are serious about your business and committed to providing high-quality products or services.

Create Customer Loyalty: A strong brand can help you create customer loyalty. When customers are loyal to your brand, they are more likely to buy from you again and recommend your business to others.

Differentiate Your Business: In a crowded market, a strong brand can help you stand out from the competition. A well-defined brand can help you communicate what makes your business unique and why customers should choose you over other options.

Increase Revenue: A strong brand can help you increase revenue. When customers are loyal to your brand, they are more likely to buy from you again and again. This can lead to increased sales and higher revenue over time.

Tips for Building a Strong Brand

Building a strong brand takes time and effort, but it's worth it in the long run. Here are some tips to help you create a brand that can withstand the test of time:

Define Your Brand: Start by defining your brand. This includes creating a mission statement, identifying your target audience, and defining your brand personality.

Create a Consistent Look and Feel: Your brand should have a consistent look and feel across all channels. This includes your logo, website, social media channels, and any other marketing materials.

Be Authentic: Authenticity is key when it comes to building a strong brand. Be true to your values and mission, and don't try to be something you're not.

Provide Excellent Customer Service: Providing excellent

customer service is one of the best ways to build a strong brand. Make sure your customers feel valued and appreciated, and always go above and beyond to exceed their expectations.

Build Relationships: Building relationships with your customers is essential for building a strong brand. Engage with them on social media, respond to their comments and questions, and show them that you care about their needs.

Monitor Your Reputation: Your brand's reputation is everything. Monitor what people are saying about your brand online, and respond to any negative comments or reviews in a professional and timely manner.

Building a strong brand is essential for long-term financial success. By establishing credibility, creating customer loyalty, differentiating your business, and increasing revenue, a strong brand can help you achieve your financial goals. By following the tips outlined in this chapter, you can create a brand that can withstand the test of time and help you achieve long-term financial success.

Disclaimer: The information provided in this book is for educational and informational purposes only. The author and publisher are not responsible for any consequences that may arise from the use of the information contained in this book. The reader should consult with a professional before making any decisions based on the information provided in this book. The author and publisher make no representations or warranties with respect to the accuracy or completeness of the contents of this book and specifically disclaim any implied warranties of merchantability or fitness for a particular purpose. The author and publisher shall not be liable for any damages or injuries whatsoever arising out of the use or inability to use the information contained in this book.

Bibliography

- Allen, Robert G. "Creating Wealth: Retire in Ten Years Using Allen's Seven Principles of Wealth." Simon and Schuster, 2006.

- Ferriss, Timothy. "The 4-Hour Work Week: Escape 9-5, Live Anywhere, and Join the New Rich." Harmony, 2007.

- Flynn, Pat. "Will It Fly? How to Test Your Next Business Idea So You Don't Waste Your Time and Money." CreateSpace Independent Publishing Platform, 2016.

- Gerber, Michael E. "The E-Myth Revisited: Why Most Small Businesses Don't Work and What to Do About It." HarperCollins, 1995.

- Godin, Seth. "Purple Cow: Transform Your Business by Being Remarkable." Portfolio, 2003.

- Halbert, Gary C. "The Boron Letters." Bond, 2013.

- Kiyosaki, Robert T. "Rich Dad Poor Dad: What the Rich Teach Their Kids About Money That the Poor and Middle Class Do Not!" Plata, 2017.

- Pennington, Tom. "The Lazy Man's Guide to Investing: How to Grow Your Wealth Without Any Work." CreateSpace Independent Publishing Platform, 2014.

- Port, Michael. "Book Yourself Solid: The Fastest, Easiest, and Most Reliable System for Getting More Clients Than You Can Handle Even if You Hate Marketing and Selling." Wiley, 2010.

- Ramsey, Dave. "The Total Money Makeover: A Proven Plan for Financial Fitness." Thomas Nelson, 2013.

- Richards, Carl. "The One-Page Financial Plan: A Simple Way to Be Smart About Your Money." Portfolio, 2015.

- Schaub, Greg, and Ruth Schaub. "Real Estate Note Investing: Using Mortgage Notes to Passively and Massively Increase Your Income." CreateSpace Independent Publishing Platform, 2014.

- Sethi, Ramit. "I Will Teach You to Be Rich." Workman, 2009.

- Stone, Brad. "The Everything Store: Jeff Bezos and the Age of Amazon." Little, Brown and Company, 2013.

- Vaynerchuk, Gary. "Crush It!: Why Now Is the Time to Cash in on Your Passion." HarperCollins, 2009.

www.ingramcontent.com/pod-product-compliance
Lightning Source LLC
Chambersburg PA
CBHW070857220526
45466CB00005B/2018